GLORY IN THE CROSS

GLORY
IN THE CROSS

A STUDY IN ATONEMENT

by

LEON MORRIS

A CANTERBURY BOOK

BAKER BOOK HOUSE
Grand Rapids, Michigan

ISBN: 0-8010-6070-2

Canterbury Books (series editor, Philip E. Hughes) are written by Anglican (Episcopalian) authors and offered as contributions of authentic Anglican thought and theology. The series will include important reprints as well as works by contemporary scholars. The significance of the subject matter, together with the quality of the writing and the reputation of the writers, is expected to ensure a wide readership for **Canterbury Books** not only among Episcopalians, but also among Christians of all denominations.

Philip Edgcumbe Hughes, Anglican scholar and author, is currently Associate Rector of St. John's Episcopal Church, Huntingdon Valley, Pennsylvania, and Visiting Professor at Westminster Theological Seminary, Philadelphia. Previously, he served in England as Vice-Principal of Tyndale Hall, Bristol; Executive Secretary of the Church Society; and Editor of *The Churchman.*

PHOTOLITHOPRINTED BY CUSHING - MALLOY, INC.
ANN ARBOR, MICHIGAN, UNITED STATES OF AMERICA
1979

INTRODUCTION

'WHEN we speak of the centrality of the Atonement', wrote P. T. Forsyth over fifty years ago, 'we mean much more, worlds more, than its place in a religious system. We are speaking of that which is the centre, not of thought, but of actual life, conscience, history, and destiny. We speak of what is the life power of the moral world and its historic crisis, the ground of the Church's existence, and the sole meaning of Christ Himself. Christ is to us just what His cross is. ... You do not understand Christ till you understand His cross' (*The Cruciality of the Cross*, pp. 25 f.).

The purpose of Dr. Leon Morris's study is precisely this, to help us to understand the cross of Christ and the reason for its centrality in the Christian faith. In his two important books *The Apostolic Preaching of the Cross* and *The Cross in the New Testament* he has already written much more extensively on this great theme. The present work is of a more popular character. The study of it will doubtless stimulate many to move on to the reading of the larger volumes.

In a day when many even in the Church are questioning the central doctrines of the historic faith, including the sovereign otherness of God, the deity of Christ, the saving efficacy of His death, and the reality of His resurrection from the dead, it is right and necessary that we should be reminded that 'a Christianity which is not cross-centred is not Christianity at all'. It was another distinguished theologian of the cross, James Denney, who insisted that the Atonement meets not only human need but also divine necessity, so that in the very act of forgiving sin God is seen to act in a manner consistent with His whole character. 'It is the recognition of this divine necessity—not to forgive, but to forgive in a way which shows that God is irreconcilable to evil, and can never treat it as other or less than it is—it is the recognition of this divine necessity, or the failure to recognize it, which ultimately divides interpreters of Christianity into evangelical and non-evangelical, those who are true to the New Testament and those who cannot digest it' (*The Atonement and the Modern Mind*, 3rd edn., 1910, p. 82).

Dr. Morris is in the succession of those who belong to the former category. While taking into account the varied theological interpretations of the cross and assigning to each its due value, he is concerned to to set forth a view of the Atonement which is consistent with the divine character: a view which, while it magnifies the love of God also vindicates His holiness and shows Him to be at once a just God and a Saviour. This, after all, is the heart of the gospel. This is the glory of the cross.

PHILIP E. HUGHES

FRANK COLQUHOUN

Joint Editors

CONTENTS

	Page
Introduction	5
1. THE MODERN OBJECTION	9
2. THE NEED FOR ATONEMENT	25
3. SIN AND SUFFERING	37
4. THE INITIATIVE IS GOD'S	46
5. CHRIST MEETS OUR NEED	58
6. OUR RESPONSE	82

CHAPTER ONE

THE MODERN OBJECTION

'Most people would genuinely *like* to believe the Christmas story, but wonder whether it *can* be true with the world as it is after nearly two thousand years. But in the case of the Atonement they ask with some impatience how anything done two thousand years ago on the Cross *could* "affect me now".'[1]

So comments the Bishop of Woolwich on the difference he sees between the attitudes of men today to the Christmas story and the atonement. The former, though incredible, is attractive. It is a beautiful story. It revives nostalgic memories of pictures on Christmas cards, of the joy of little children, of the ideal of 'Peace on earth, goodwill towards men'. To be sure, men do not quite see how the Son of God (if there be a God) *could* have been born among men. To men brought up in a scientific age the whole concept bristles with difficulties. But they are not repelled when Christians say He was. They may regard Christians as hopelessly credulous, as all too ready to believe what they want to believe. But they would genuinely like to be convinced on this point.

[1] *Honest to God* (London, 1963), pp. 78 f.

The story is attractive and they would like to think there are grounds for believing it. It would round off the Christmas festivities nicely!

But the atonement is different. Here there are no stars leading wise men, nor Christmas trees, nor any equivalent of 'Peace on earth'. The Church, it is true, talks about the forgiveness of sins that Christ won by His death, and about the mighty victory of Easter. But to the man in the street this carries no conviction. He does not see himself as a sinner, he is not at all worried about the sins the Church says may be forgiven, and he sees no necessity for being saved from them. And as for the 'victory of Easter', what does that mean? The important thing about Easter for him is that it is a holiday.

The story behind it, he feels, is incredible. And it is not only incredible, it is unattractive. Modern man does not see how Christ's death a couple of thousand years ago could save him now, and he does not want to see it. If there is any saving to be done he prefers to do it himself. He does not like to think that his eternal destiny depends on what a Galilean carpenter did for him so long ago. He rejects the incarnation, but does so with some regret. It would be nice if it were true. But he rejects the atonement with a touch of exasperation. There is nothing 'nice' about it. It is not something that men want to believe. It is something on which the Church insists and which they find merely irritating.

There is nothing attractive about the cross. The real cross, I mean. It is possible to make beautiful little jewelled crosses as sparkling ornaments for ladies to wear. But the cross on which Christ was crucified was an instrument of execution. It was a gibbet. It was ugly and cruel and bloody. The modern world finds it completely repulsive.

The world might perhaps find it acceptable if it were allowed to interpret it in its own way. We think we understand heroism (even if we are not particularly heroic ourselves) and we admire those who endure misunderstanding, betrayal and death in a good cause. We do not mind seeing the cross as, for example, a notable act of self-sacrifice. We think of the heroism in suffering of say, a Father Damien, or even a non-Christian like Gandhi, and many another. Such men have sacrificed themselves for their fellows. They have endured hardship and misery so that others might receive the benefit. They have died that others might live in the fullest sense. If the cross may be seen as another heroic act of martyrdom, to be set alongside these, then the modern world can come to terms with it.

But orthodox Christians have never seen it in those terms. They recognize, of course, that the cross was an act of self-sacrifice. On the cross Jesus Christ set an example of patient suffering. He became our pattern, showing how we should behave in trying circumstances. There is a quiet heroism in all that

He did as He was rejected by His people and cruelly done to death.

But believers have always said more than this. They have maintained that Christians are 'redeemed' men. They have delighted to speak of Christ as 'Saviour'. They have taught that what happened on the cross has lasting effects for the salvation of all who put their trust in Jesus Christ. Indeed, they have gone further. They have maintained that unless a man puts his trust in Christ, unless he has been redeemed by what Christ did for him in dying on Calvary, then he is not, in the New Testament sense, a Christian at all.

Throughout the centuries the Christian Church has steadfastly held that the cross is at the very centre of the Christian faith. It has taken the cross as the symbol of Christianity, and this advisedly. It has seen the cross not as one of many things that equally go to make up the Christian faith, but as that which alone gives meaning to the whole. On the cross the purpose of God is summed up. On the cross the purpose of God is worked out as it is worked out nowhere else.

It is with this that the modern world takes issue. As the Bishop of Woolwich says, to many of our contemporaries it is frankly incredible that anything done in Galilee a couple of thousand years ago could have any effect on men here and now in Africa or in Asia, in Europe or in America or in Australia. Men do not see how the Christian doctrine can be true. And therefore they reject it out of hand.

In the face of this attitude it must be said gently perhaps, but nevertheless quite firmly, that truth and the ideas of modern men are not necessarily to be equated. A thing is not guaranteed to be true because most men today believe it. Nor is it necessarily untrue because most men today do not believe it. As a matter of historical fact, most beliefs accepted by men in every previous generation are no longer held to be true in this scientific age. And there is every likelihood that the verdict of posterity on many of the beliefs of this our day and generation will not be dissimilar.

This means that we require some criterion other than the views of twentieth century man when we come to assess the truth or otherwise of the Christian doctrine of the atonement. Whether or not we accept the orthodox Christian belief that the Bible is the final authority, and that it conveys to us God's supreme revelation to man, we need something more than 'This the modern world thinks!' We cannot allow ourselves to be subject to the whims and prejudices of a particular age, not even our own.

This is the first point I want to make. It may well be true, as the Bishop of Woolwich says, that the modern world finds the Christian doctrine of the atonement incredible. But this does not in fact make it incredible. Admittedly it means that Christians who live in the modern world ought to take another look at it. They may have been too ready to accept traditional beliefs. The scepticism of their fellows may well be the means of directing their attention to some objections to the belief that they have not considered, or have not considered sufficiently. The traditional formulations of the Church are not necessarily sacrosanct. It is the duty (and the privilege) of each succeeding generation of Christians to examine them afresh in the endeavour to discover whether the advance of knowledge generally has any light to shed on the way the faith has been formulated. If this proves that the faith has been wrongly expressed then the doctrine should be revised or in the extreme case abandoned.

But in any reconstruction of Christian doctrine we need some criterion other than the consensus of opinion in a given day and age. The voice of the multitude has too often been proved false as well as fickle for us to take it as a final standard now. And if we look again at modern achievements in such realms as ethics we may well hesitate even longer before according this generation the privilege of being accounted the definitive interpreters of Christianity.

THE BABE OF BETHLEHEM

The comment of the Bishop of Woolwich with which we started lays it down that most ordinary people today would like to think that the Christmas story is true. But not only the ordinary non-Christian is interested in this story. Many of our most serious theologians see in the story of the Babe of Bethlehem the central truth of Christianity. I do not, of course, mean that they stake everything on the details of the story as recorded in the Gospels. I mean rather that they lay all their emphasis on the incarnation. They hold that the great truth of Christianity is that in the fulness of time God became man. God sent His Son into the world to make the complete and final revelation of Himself, and of what we ought to be.

Theologians of this kind remind us that from of old God has made Himself known to men in all kinds of ways. Quite apart from the revelation apparent in nature He spoke through the prophets, and before them through the law-givers and the psalmists. He revealed Himself also in the 'mighty deeds' recorded in the Old Testament, but more especially in the events surrounding the call of Abraham, the Exodus, and the Exile. Last of all and supremely He revealed Himself through His son.

Seen in this way the coming of Jesus is essentially an act of revelation. It puts the seal on all the imperfect and partial revelations that had been made before. It shows us what God is like and what love is like. It challenges us to learn to love the God who reveals Himself and to model our lives on the perfect life of the carpenter of Nazareth.

This stress on the incarnation takes very seriously

God's purpose to make Himself known to men. In itself it is not at all incompatible, of course, with the orthodox Christian belief in the atonement. Indeed, it is a necessary presupposition of that belief. Unless the One who died on the cross was none less than the incarnate Son of God the atonement is meaningless and impossible. No one who was merely a man could bring the supreme blessing to other men by his death. No mere man could bear the sins of the world as he died. Thus it has always been a most important part of the Christian faith that the very Son of God came to earth and lived among men before laying down His perfect life on the cross. There is no kind of antagonism between the incarnation and the atonement. They go together. The atonement is not possible without the incarnation.

But it is possible so to dwell on the incarnation as to leave no real place for the atonement. Some, for example, have seen in the incarnation nothing save evidence that God and man are closely related, and a basis for stressing the immanence of God in this world. Others have thought of the incarnation as showing us that God is deeply interested in human life and have accordingly made the incarnation the basis of an all-absorbing interest in human culture. Yet others use the doctrine as a basis for a profound interest in the sacraments, which are thought of as 'the extension of the incarnation'. It cannot be denied that the results of a preoccupation with the incarnation may be various. And it may lead to a neglect of the atonement. The cross may be seen as nothing more than the fitting completion in sacrifice of the one perfect life.

A corollary which is often drawn is that too much emphasis has been put on the death of Jesus. Thus a theologian like G. S. Hendry can say concerning Jesus' death, 'Its nonuniqueness is an implicate of the incarnation.'[2] He sees the death of Jesus as much like the death of other men. It is the life which is different and which is the significant thing.

One unexpected consequence of this (which I have tried to draw out elsewhere[3]) is that the death of Christ is not seen as doing anything in particular for men. This appears to follow from its nonuniqueness. But, interestingly, when it is all boiled down, the life of Jesus, on which Hendry puts his stress, does not seem to do anything either. While he is insistent that the life of Jesus is tremendously important he is also insistent that what saves men is the grace of God. Men were saved by God's grace before Jesus came, so that nothing that Jesus did is to be thought of as *essential*. Jesus came to reveal the way more perfectly, but it was not a new way. It was basically the same way as before, with forgiveness coming by the same grace of the same God.

[2] *The Gospel of the Incarnation* (Philadelphia, 1958), p. 143.
[3] *The Cross in the New Testament* (Grand Rapids and Exeter, 1965), pp. 375 ff.

17

It is true that the whole Christian message must always be seen against the background of the Old Testament. And it is also true that the teaching of Jesus is continuous with that of the prophets. But when full allowance has been made for this, Hendry's position is calamitous. It means that Jesus really did nothing for us at all. If men could be forgiven before He came and quite independently of anything that He did, then men can still be forgiven in the same way. In the end this view means that not only is the death of Jesus robbed of significance, but the life, on which all the emphasis is placed, likewise appears to have little meaning.

It would not be true to say that all who have put their emphasis on the incarnation would be prepared to follow Professor Hendry in all his views. But I have drawn attention to him because he is one of the most recent and one of the abler exponents of this emphasis, and because he has argued his case so persuasively. Those who stress the incarnation and refuse to go along with him may perhaps be fairly criticized on the grounds that they do not see the logic of their position as clearly as he does. For once we take the significance from the death of Jesus and emphasize instead the incarnation we are shut up to the view that what Christ came to do was to reveal the Father. His function was purely revelatory. This may mean that He can show us the way of salvation. It may even mean that He can show it more clearly than others. But it cannot mean that He is *necessary* to our salvation.

A strong emphasis on the incarnation is legitimate, and indeed necessary on biblical premises. But when it is taken to the point of emptying the death of Christ of its saving significance what is left is not Christian. It may have a high-sounding scholarly or ecclesiastical ring. But it is not authentic Christianity.

Christians traditionally have seen in Jesus One whom they can call 'Saviour'. They have believed that He died to bring them a salvation they could not obtain of themselves. Remove this and you have taken away the distinctive thing from Christianity. You have robbed it of its power.

RETRIBUTION

Another objection to the atonement often urged in recent times takes its rise from modern views on punishment. Nowadays it is widely denied that punishment is retributory. Instead it is insisted that it must be seen as deterrent or as reformatory. There are vigorous discussions as to the relative places of these two aspects of punishment, and as to whether we need them both in a satisfying understanding of the subject. But it many circles there is no longer any serious attention paid to the idea that punishment is retributive.

Now the Christian idea of the atonement, it is pointed out, involves the acceptance of the idea that sin *ought* to be punished. Take away this retributive idea and, it is claimed, no meaning can be put into the expression, 'Christ died to bear our sins'. Since the basic view of punishment is wrong, the whole superstructure is faulty.

Like the first view we were looking at, this one rests on the premise that what appears true to modern men must be accepted without further ado. In this case there is the added consideration that in the past retribution has often been stressed to such an extent that the reformation of the sinner has been lost sight of. When it is possible to draw attention to the harmful consequences which have followed from the rigid application of the theory of retribution without regard to other considerations, plausibility is given to the contention that the whole retributive theory is wrong.

But this does not follow. And in any case where either of the other views is taken as the whole story, harmful consequences also follow (as I hope to show in a later chapter). No one view is sufficient for the human situation, when taken by itself. It is only the retributive view which introduces the note of justice into punishment. Apart from this view there is nothing to limit the activities of the would-be deterrers or reformers. This, of itself, is surely sufficient to demonstrate that retribution is not to be simply dismissed. While it must be supplemented from the other views it cannot be abandoned.

This truth seems clearer to our literary giants than to the community at large. It is a striking fact, and one which should be considered in its bearing on the atonement more often than it is, that the greatest literature is tragedy. There are some fine comedies. But by common consent those writings in the world's literature which really plumb man's nature to the depths are the great tragedies.

Now a tragedy is always the working out of the consequences of a sin. As long as all the characters are acting honourably and doing the things they should, there is no room for tragedy to operate. But sooner or later the writer introduces a character who has done something he ought not to have done, or perhaps who has left undone something that he should have done (there are sins of omission as well as of commission). The effect of this on the life of the sinner and on the lives of others then forms the matter of the tragedy. It is impossible for the wrong simply to fade away. That is the basic fact that creates the tragedy. Unexpiated sin obstinately refuses to efface itself. It continues, and it wreaks havoc.

The biblical doctrine of the atonement starts from this basic fact. Despite the shallow optimism of some modern thinkers, sin cannot simply be ignored. It must be dealt with or it will reap a grim harvest. The present state of the world is a vivid commentary on this fact.

The consequences of sin here and now are serious enough. Most of the ills we see among men are due in the last resort to sin of some sort. Most obviously the pains and discomforts brought by war are the result of the sin of not living at peace. This entails physical suffering on a wide scale. But it also involves mental and other kinds of suffering, and these may result also from causes other than war. Wherever there is disunity there is attendant strife and unhappiness.

And so we could go on. Throughout our community whenever we find suffering (apart from that caused by disease) we can usually find sin of some kind behind it. And the other side of the coin is that all sin has some unpleasant consequence. It will not die.

Now if in the affairs of men sin cannot simply be wiped out, why should we think that this will be the case where God is concerned? It is unthinkable that the God of the Bible should condone wrongdoing. He is all-holy. The prophet could pray, 'Thou art of purer eyes than to behold evil, and canst not look on iniquity' (Hab. 1:13). Such a God will not be complacent about evil.

This does not mean that He will not forgive the sinner. It is the consistent teaching of the Bible that He can and will do this. But it is also the consistent teaching of the Bible that forgiveness is not a truism.

It cannot be assumed. Indeed on the surface of things the probabilities are all against it. There is every reason for thinking that sin matters to God. And in the last resort it is God's word, not man's, that is decisive. He is the Creator. He is the Lawgiver. He lays down the conditions. It is for us to hear and obey.

In the Bible forgiveness is always regarded as something wonderful. The sinner could expect nothing other than punishment. But God, infinitely powerful and infinitely full of grace, has acted to put man's sin away. The consistent picture throughout the Bible is that God provides the means for man's forgiveness. If it appears that man would never have guessed what would be necessary, and if in the end we are left with some questions still remaining, that should not surprise us. After all, the situation is a complex one, and sinful men do not know really what are the conditions under which sin may be expiated. They know that unless sin is expiated it will reap a grim harvest. They know also that God is a God of love and that He will bring men back to Him. And they will be content to accept God's way in all this.

It is this, then, that is our concern in this book. We shall look at what the Bible has to say about the plight of man, and about the way in which God makes provision for forgiveness. In this first chapter we have been concerned simply to notice that a number of modern 'solutions' to the problem are far too easy. They fail to reckon with the seriousness of sin and with the seriousness with which God takes sin.

Any treatment of the subject that has any claim at all to being satisfactory must take account of God's hatred of all that is evil, together with His complete readiness to forgive. These two facts, taken together, make for a complicated situation. Let us not expect then that the Bible teaching on the subject will be easy. It is not superficial. It deals with realities. To understand it requires careful thought. But thought on this subject is abundantly worth-while. For here is the deep, basic subject of all religion. How can sinful man become acceptable before a holy God?

The Christian answer is that this can be brought about only through what God Himself has done in Christ.

CHAPTER TWO

THE NEED FOR ATONEMENT

'THE Egyptian viewed his misdeeds not as sins, but as aberrations.' So writes Professor H. Frankfort,[1] and puts his finger on a characteristic of much religion in the ancient world. It was true of many besides the Egyptians that misdeeds were seen as aberrations, but not sins. In emphatic contrast, however, it is characteristic of Old Testament religion that misdeeds were seen as sins, not as aberrations. That is to say, they were seen primarily as offences against God, not as regrettable minor idiosyncrasies more or less harmful to man. They represented a failure to conform to the standards God had laid down and to which He expected man to conform.

This has important consequences. If we may cite Frankfort again: 'the theme of God's wrath is practically unknown in Egyptian literature; for the Egyptian, in his aberrations, is not a sinner whom God rejects but an ignorant man who is disciplined and corrected.'[2] Not only the Egyptian, but most

---

[1] Cited in *The Old Testament Against Its Environment* (London, 1950), by G. Ernest Wright, p. 106.
[2] *Loc. cit.*

people of the ancient world would have agreed that man is in no great danger because of his misdeeds. It was often felt that service to the gods was praiseworthy and that a man must be careful lest he incur the displeasure of a god. But this is a different thing altogether from seeing offences as sins and seeing them as contrary to the will of the one righteous God. For the pagan world in general the gods were capricious. One had to take care to keep in their good books, but this did not necessarily mean that one had to live an upright life. These gods of the heathen were not moral gods, and there was no particular reason why their worshippers should be moral men.

It was quite otherwise with Israel and the God of Israel. God was seen as a righteous God, and a God concerned that His people should also be righteous. This meant that if His people departed from the ways of God, rebelling against His commandments, they could expect the strongest reaction from His side. They called this 'the wrath of God'. The expression is not in high favour in these days and some theologians go so far as to suggest that we should discard it altogether. But it corresponds to a reality and it is the biblical phrase. If we are to think of God as a righteous God we must accept the thought that He reacts against evil in His people. He does not regard it lightly but opposes it with all the strength of His holy nature. That is why the Old Testament has so much to say about the sin of man and the attitude of God to it. It is not an unimportant issue. It is something of critical importance. Unless something can be done about either the sin or the wrath man is in no good state.

Let us first notice that in Scripture, in both Old and New Testaments, there is the consistent teaching that we are all in this together. It is recorded that as Solomon prayed his great prayer at the dedication of the temple he said, 'there is no man that sinneth not' (I Ki. 8:46). We have almost the same thing said in another place, 'there is not a just man upon earth, that doeth good, and sinneth not' (Eccl. 7:20). There are several passages in the Psalms which are relevant. From them we select but two: 'there is none that doeth good, no, not one' (Ps. 14:3); 'for in thy sight shall no man living be justified' (Ps. 143:2).

Passages of this kind could be multiplied in the Old Testament. It is clear that the prophets in particular were very depressed about the amount of wrongdoing they saw among the people. They thundered their denunciations against an evil people and warned men that it was not enough to find their conduct approved by the general standards of their day. If they had transgressed the law of God they were sinners. The prophets had not the slightest doubt but that the wrath of God would be visited upon them. The question was only 'When?' not 'Whether?'

It has often been pointed out that the ethical

vocabulary of the Old Testament is very rich and that, specifically, there is a great variety of words for sin. Some students of the Old Testament have gone to considerable trouble to enumerate and classify them. They point out that some have meanings like 'to miss the mark' or 'to go astray', while others deal with the effects of sin either in its badness or moral worthlessness or the like, or in its effect on the sinner, namely, that it makes him guilty. However, most are agreed that the really significant Old Testament words in this connection are those which represent sin as essentially 'rebellion'. Whatever else may be said about sin, it is always a defiance of God's good and perfect will. It is thus a rebellion on the part of sinful man against his Creator. It is this which makes sin the heinous thing that it is in the Old Testament and which ensures that in due time it will receive fit punishment.

There is nothing different when we turn to the New Testament. St. Paul assures us that 'all have sinned, and come short of the glory of God' (Rom. 3:23). It is worth noting that his verb 'come short' is not in the past tense as the English might perhaps indicate. It is in the present tense. Paul is saying first that all have at some time sinned, and secondly, that day by day they still come short of God's glory. He is laying it down that sin is not simply an event in the past. It is a reality of present life which we all know only too well.

This kind of teaching is not confined to the great apostle. Our Lord himself could say, 'If ye then, being evil. . . .' (Mt. 7:11). He quietly assumes that men are all sinners. It is a point which He finds it unnecessary to argue.

We could reinforce this point with further quotation as when John says, 'If we say that we have no sin, we deceive ourselves, and the truth is not in us' (1 Jn. 1:8). But more impressive than the quotation of individual passages is the nature of the positive righteousness which is enjoined in the New Testament. If we look at the kind of life Jesus expects us to live we see with frightening clarity how far short we come of what we ought to be.

A. M. Hunter brings it out in this way: 'From time to time one hears people declare that they "like" the Sermon on the Mount. It is in fact the most terrible indictment of human nature in all literature. . . Who is sufficient for these merciless moral demands? Who is able to fulfil them? Not Tolstoi or any other. If that is the ideal, God have mercy on us all, sinners.'[3]

Not dissimilar from the people to whom Hunter refers are those who suggest that the theologians are complicating life for ordinary Christians. All that is necessary, we are told, is that people should live 'according to the simple teaching of the Sermon on the Mount'. Anyone who says this kind of thing

[3] *The Unity of the New Testament* (London, 1944), pp. 84 f.

has almost certainly not read the Sermon, or if he has, has not paid attention to it. Consider some of the things it says. Jesus tells us that it is not enough to refrain from murdering people in accordance with the Sixth Commandment. We break the spirit of this Commandment if we are angry with another without a just cause. Again, it is not enough to refrain from the overt act of adultery. Even the lustful look breaks this particular commandment. And so on. As we go through the Sermon the point is driven home that our lives are expected to be lived on the very highest plane. If there were any doubt about this the Sermon itself removes it: 'Be ye therefore perfect, even as your Father which is in heaven is perfect' (Mt. 5:48).

Now the terrible thing about all this is that Jesus appears to be completely serious. He really means that we should *never* engage in unrighteous anger, that we should *never* cast the lustful look. He really means that our lives should be lived in complete perfection. We should not delude ourselves into thinking that a comfortable easy standard is all that is required. It is not. God expects us to raise our standards to perfection, and we are accountable when we do not do this.

THE SERIOUSNESS OF SIN

Let us look further at this accountability. Not only does Jesus teach us that we are all sinners, not only does He make us realize this from the positive nature of the righteousness He demands, but He insists that it is a serious matter when we do not reach the standard He lays down. We find it difficult to enter into this aspect of His thought, because to us sin does not appear to be terribly serious.

An instructive example of the difference between the way we look at sin and the way He regarded it is found in the story of the healing of the paralytic who was carried to Jesus by four of his friends. Unable to approach Jesus because of the crowds they went up the stairs on the outside of the house where He was, made a hole in the roof over His head, and lowered their friend down in front of the Lord. Their determined action was the measure of their earnest desire that their friend might be cured. But it is interesting to see that Jesus at first neglected the man's physical condition. He said to him, 'Son, thy sins be forgiven thee' (Mk. 2:5). Only after He had dealt with the sin did He proceed to cure the man.

It is not difficult to imagine the outcry that would arise at the present time if any Christian man suggested that we ought to deal with the spiritual need of an invalid before doing anything to alleviate his suffering. But that is just what Jesus did. To Him the sin was the really serious thing. Treating that could not wait. The bodily condition was different. That could wait until the thing of major importance was dealt with.

It is in line with this that Jesus' whole ministry was one to sinners. He did not come to minister to righteous people but to call sinners to repentance (Mk. 2:17; Lk. 19:10). He thought that outward defilements mattered very little compared with the sinful things which really do defile the whole man (Mt. 15:19 f.). To be a sinner is to be a slave (Jn. 8:34), and concerning one specific sin, that of Judas, Jesus said, 'good were it for that man if he had never been born' (Mk. 14:21). He could even go so far as to say, 'he that shall blaspheme against the Holy Ghost hath never forgiveness' (Mk. 3:29). We should not let disputes as to the exact nature of this sin blind us to the fact that Jesus is stressing its extreme seriousness. In line with this we should take His references to hell fire (Mt. 5:22–29 etc.) It is not always realized that Jesus spoke more often of hell than of heaven. For Him the consequences of unforgiven sin were terrible to contemplate.

Similarly Paul can say 'the wages of sin is death' (Rom. 6:23), and again 'the wrath of God is revealed from heaven against all ungodliness and unrighteousness of men' (Rom. 1:18).

These quotations could without difficulty be very greatly multiplied. It is plain to the New Testament writers both that man is a sinner and that sin is serious. Very little in the Bible can be understood until this point is grasped.

One difficulty that modern men often have in trying to understand their position as the Bible lays it down arises from their failure to reckon with the fact that God is the Judge. This is simple enough when it is pointed out. But so often in our thinking we assume that what seems right and good to us is what will ultimately prevail. Without putting it into words we regard it as unthinkable that the consensus of opinion at the present time could possibly be wildly astray.

Now when we deal with ultimate reality we must recognize that it is God's word, not man's, that is decisive. It is God who is the final Judge, not man. It is God's demands which are significant in this situation, not man's estimate of his own position. This point cannot be too frequently or too strongly emphasized. Our generation seems to have lost sight of it completely. But it is fundamental to any right understanding of the position.

Let me take a homely illustration. If I go along to a football match and discover that the charge for admittance is say, five shillings, I may object furiously. I may say to the man at the gate, 'I know both those teams. Neither of them is capable of a good performance. They could not possibly put on a game which would be worth five shillings to see. I'll pay two!' But no matter how firmly I hold this point of view I cannot impose it on the gatekeeper. If I argue with him along these lines he will have nothing to do with me. In fact there are only two courses open to me. I can pay the five shillings and go in and see the match or I can keep my money and stay out. What I cannot do is to fix an admittance charge that satisfies me, pay that, and go in. It is not my right to fix the admittance charge. I can take it or leave it. But I cannot modify it.

There is a parallel in the spiritual realm. It is God's heaven not ours. He lays down the terms of admittance, not we. We can enter on God's terms, or we can stay out. What we cannot do is to impose our own conditions on God.

That is why is is such a terrible thing that men in our day so often without reference to the Bible or to the Church or to anything other than themselves assure us airily that they are all right. Their lives are not too bad, they inform us, so that when they stand before God things will work out. This is the fundamental error. It means a refusal to take God seriously and a determination to try and impose our will on Him.

It cannot be done. God is no man's tool. He does what is right in His own sight. And if we are wise when we are thinking about eternal issues we will realize where the final say lies. We can get nowhere in our study of the atonement until we realize that it is God's estimate of the situation which is decisive and not ours. And the New Testament makes it abundantly plain that God is displeased with every act of sin. The Lord is opposed to all evil whether in you or in me or in anyone else. He has laid it down that nothing and no one that defiles will ever enter His heaven (Rev. 21:27).

From all this it is plain enough that man's sin has left him in no good case. He has offended against the law of God, and has shut himself out from the sphere of God's blessing. It is possible for this state of affairs to be reversed. Salvation is a reality. But it does not come by merely human effort.

The Anglican Church makes this very plain. Article XI assures us that 'We are accounted righteous before God, only for the merit of our Lord and Saviour Jesus Christ by Faith, and not for our own works or deservings'. This truth is brought out elsewhere. Article XVIII, for example, says 'They also are to be had accursed that presume to say, That every man shall be saved by the Law or Sect which he professeth, so that he be diligent to frame his life according to that Law, and the light of Nature. For holy Scripture doth set out unto us only the Name of Jesus Christ, whereby men must be saved.'

More could be quoted from the Prayer Book to the same effect. The compilers of the Book of Common Prayer constantly bore in mind that Christ's atoning work, and that alone, is the means of our salvation. They consistently exclude the possibility that man's own efforts can bring him salvation.

That is why there is a need for atonement. Our

good deeds, if we have any, present no problem. They represent the ideal we should attain day by day.

But our evil deeds do present a problem. It is more than difficult for anyone who takes moral issues seriously to see how sinful men can ever rest in heaven with a righteous and holy God. There is the problem. God is holy. We are not.

In that situation God Himself provides the remedy.

CHAPTER THREE

SIN AND SUFFERING

'PUNISHMENT must be essentially reformatory.' This dogma is usually accepted unquestioningly by modern students of the problem. In a subsidiary aspect punishment is seen also as a deterrent. But nothing must be allowed to conflict with the sacred dictum that reform is the significant thing in the punishment of anyone, and especially of criminals. Certainly retribution has no place in an enlightened society.

This dogma, however, is contradicted by a common notion, held deep down by most of us, that sin *ought* to be punished. When we hear of a particularly revolting crime we say something like, 'Boiling in oil is too good for that fellow!'

Why do we say such things? Basically because we believe that sin or crime ought to be punished. It is not a question of whether the criminal will or will not be reformed. It is not a question of whether punishing him will or will not deter others from doing the same sort of thing. Both these factors are relevant and none of us would suggest that they should be forgotten. But our conviction that boiling in oil is too good for the vicious criminal who has offended our tender susceptibilities does not arise from either. It arises from the view that there is a natural connection between sin and suffering. The sin *ought* to be punished.

The view that punishment is retribution is very much out of favour at present, especially among our penologists. This is quite understandable. Penologists are practical men. Their concern is not with abstract questions of right and wrong. Rather they face the question of what should be done in the concrete cases of the specific criminals who are before them. They want to see these men and women rehabilitated and returned to society as upright, law-abiding members of the community. Criminals have somehow picked up anti-social tendencies which have led them into anti-social patterns of behaviour. The important thing it seems, is to correct them, to eliminate the anti-social patterns and to make it possible for every man to fill his appointed niche. The huge expenditure on those penal institutions where criminals are simply locked away from society, they feel, might be better spent. It ought to be channelled into institutions from which society would get a better return for its money, institutions which would reform the criminals and make them into model citizens.

Anything that helps to break down the criminals' bad habits is welcomed. Anything that engenders better behaviour is sought out. The over-riding concern for the reformation of the criminal makes the penologists tender to those forms of treatment (we can scarcely call them 'punishment') which do in fact reform. By contrast they view with the gravest suspicion any form of punishment which does not lead to reformation. When they see harsh prison conditions producing habitual criminals out of men who might well have been reclaimed if properly treated, it is not at all surprising that they react against punishment which does no more than punish. They see it as brutal, degrading, and altogether unworthy of a society which claims to be civilized. It is the most natural thing in the world that such men should criticize retributive views of punishment in the strongest of terms.

Let it be said at once that enlightened penologists must be supported wholeheartedly in all their efforts to undo the ravages of a misguided past. A very high priority must be given to the devising of such forms of treatment as will reform the greatest number of criminals. Important advances have been made in this field and all men of goodwill rejoice that it is so.

And if there is much in the reformatory theories with which we must be in agreement it is also true that punishment is a deterrent. Nobody enjoys being punished. The reflection that punishment will surely follow an offence will often give the potential offender occasion to pause and then to desist from his plan. This is good for him and good for the community. There can be no doubt that one reason for punishing criminals is the effect on others.

Neither the reformatory not the deterrent theories of punishment ought to be minimized. Yet it is difficult to think that either singly or together they give the whole truth. Neither reformation nor deterrence *of itself* is sufficient as the reason behind punishment. This becomes obvious if we subject these views to examination.

Let us take deterrence first. There are occasions when deterrence does not work. A number of authorities, for example, have pointed out that the death penalty for murder is no deterrent at all. Indeed, this has been one of the principal reasons put forward by those who advocate its abolition. They point out that murder is such a serious affair that it will be committed only when a person is so deeply involved, and so oblivious of consequences, that he does not greatly care what will happen to him. Now if deterrence were the only reason for punishment the logical consequence would be to exempt murderers from penalty. Reflection might well add other offences to the list. Where it is clear that a penalty will not deter men there is, on this view, no case for penalty at all. Few would be prepared to endorse such a conclusion. Why ? Because we recognize that there is more to punishment than deterrence. Even if people will not be deterred they ought to be punished in some way when they have committed a crime.

In similar fashion it is plain that reformation will not do as the sole reason for punishment. There are some people, admittedly a minority, who are so revolted when they have committed their first crime that they cannot do any such thing again. Quite without punishment they turn away from their evil way. When there is no need for reformation, reformation having occurred already, this view ought to mean that the offender should suffer no penalty. But we all agree that it would be a curious state of affairs indeed were some people to be punished for a given offence while others were let off on the grounds that we do not think they will do it again!

Again, there are some people who are so hardened in their evil ways that no punishment seems able to turn them from them. On the view we are considering these people, too, should be released without further ado. Punishment is not going to reform them. Let them go. By contrast, as long as there is a prospect that the criminal will be reformed he ought to be kept in prison, even though his offence be minor. Yet most of us feel that for an unimportant crime the time will surely come when we must say, 'Let him go. He has been punished enough!'

Neither reformation nor deterrence will suffice as the rationale of punishment. The plain fact is that it is only ill-desert that gives the *right* to punish. Here let us notice some important words from F. R. Bradley: 'Punishment is punishment, only where it is deserved. We pay the penalty, because we owe it, and for no other reason; and if punishment is inflicted for any other reason whatever than because it is merited by wrong, it is a gross immorality, a crying injustice, an abominable crime, and not what it pretends to be. We may have regard for whatever considerations we please—our own convenience, the good of society, the benefit of the offender; we are fools, and worse, if we fail to do so. Having once the right to punish, we may modify the punishment according to the useful and the pleasant; but these are external to the matter, they cannot give us a right to punish, and nothing can do that but criminal desert.'[1]

This is a point of the utmost importance, an importance which is no whit diminished by the fact that it is often overlooked in modern discussions. It points us to a truth that deep down we all respect. There is an instinctive recognition that crime and sin deserve punishment. Whether the sinner is reformed or reformable or not, and whether a punishment will deter him and others or not he still ought to undergo punishment commensurate with his sin. If he has sinned grievously he ought to be punished severely. If he has sinned slightly he ought to be punished slightly. The only way in which a man can expiate his crime is to undergo adequate penalty.

[1] Cited by L. Hodgson: *The Doctrine of the Atonement* (London, 1951), p. 54.

The offender himself usually recognizes this. While none of us likes being punished, yet it is the case that, when our sin has been brought home to our conscience, we welcome rather than avoid penalty. Especially is this the case if our sin has brought suffering to the innocent. If the penalty can be so devised that it brings help and succour to those we have wronged we welcome it all the more.

In fact this must be recognized before penalty can have a deterrent or reformatory effect. If a man feels that his penalty is unjust, being greater than his crime deserves, then it will not serve as a deterrent, and it will not reform him. It will infuriate him or perhaps it will break him. But it will do him no good. He must be able to say, 'I, indeed, receive the just reward of my deeds', before his penalty can do him any good at all. Penalty must be felt to be deserved if it is to have adequate effect.

In an important article[2] C. S. Lewis argues that it is important *for the offender* that the retributive view of punishment be established. His point is that if the deterrent or reformatory view be held, the things done to the offender are just as compulsory as on the retributive view, though they will perhaps no longer be called punishment. But now they will not be controlled by considerations of justice. The basic question arising in the case of a reformatory

<hr>

[2] *Twentieth Century* (*Australia*), vol. III, no. 3; it was reprinted in *The Churchman* (London), vol. LXXIII, pp. 55 ff.

process is 'Will it reform ?' The offender will not be treated justly at all on these views. He will be treated on the basis of whether what is done to him will deter him (or others) or reform him. For his own protection it is important that the concept of desert be introduced. He must not be punished beyond what he deserves, however good the intentions of the deterrers or the reformers.

It is not in my judgment true that retribution is the only thing to be said about punishment. I trust that I have made this clear already. But it is the fundamental thing, and without it none of the views will stand. And in considering the atonement it is the view of punishment that is the significant one. There is that about human sin that is serious. A God who simply waved His hand and said, 'Let us forget about sin' would not be a just or a moral God. When sin has been committed it cannot simply be overlooked. The conscience of all mankind demands that it be dealt with, not overlooked.

I do not think that we can progress much beyond this point. The difficulty about our criminal codes is that we do not know exactly how to apply the law of retribution. There have been occasions when we all agree that monstrous penalties have been exacted for slight offences. There have also been occasions when outrageous crimes (especially if perpetrated by the wealthy and the influential) have gone comparatively unscathed. At best our legal systems are approximations. But in however blundering a fashion they do point us to the truth that evil ought to be punished, and that we should strive after an ever closer approximation to the ideal penalty.

And if our legal systems are imperfect, so is our knowledge of what should be done about sin. We know it ought to be punished, but we do not know precisely how. It revolts our sense of what is fitting that nothing be done about it. Or that all that should be done is that the sinner should be reformed, or deterred from sinning again. These views are too shallow by far.

Thus we are led to the Bible view that sin can be put away only by suffering. It does not wither by being ignored. It must be expiated. And expiation is costly. In this case it cost the Son of God His life. But the Bible insists that this death was necessary. The Son of man *must* suffer.

CHAPTER FOUR

THE INITIATIVE IS GOD'S

SOMETIMES in their anxiety to give due emphasis to what Christ has done for us, evangelicals have unwittingly introduced division into the Godhead. I do not think they have ever intended to do this, but the picture they have given is of a process which runs like this. Man has sinned. Because of his sin he has put himself outside the place of fellowship with God and condemned himself to hell. God, the righteous Judge, would not be true to His own nature unless He upheld the moral law and sentenced men to eternal loss. He did so. But in this situation Jesus Christ, the very Son of God, in His great love for men, came where they were, lived among them, died on Calvary's cross to put away their sins. Because of His love, and because of His readiness to die for them, they are saved.

There is an element of truth in this. But only an element. The picture of God that this gives us is of a stern Judge, one who is ready to acquiesce in a situation wherein the bulk of mankind, indeed, the whole of mankind, is lost eternally. It is only because His Son decides otherwise and acts in such a way as to bring His resolve into effect that any are saved at all.

Emphatically this is not the position taken up in the Bible. Though we must respect the motives of those who have caricatured the atonement in this fashion, we must decline to accept the picture they have drawn. It is true all men are sinners and lost. It is also true that the Son of God has intervened to save them. But it is not at all true that the Father did nothing but wait until the Son had wrought the work of salvation. The New Testament is very clear that salvation takes place only because the Father willed it so.

This is very clear whenever the New Testament writers speak of the fulfilment of prophecy, as they often do. Let us consider three instances in one chapter of St. Mark's Gospel. Jesus said, 'The Son of man indeed goeth, as it is written of him' (Mk. 14:21). This refers to His leaving this world in the death on the cross. Jesus has said that He will be betrayed and He clearly has death in mind. But He sees this death as fulfilling the ancient prophecy. It is impossible to interpret this save as meaning that the death is in line with the will of His Father, for prophecy records what He has determined to bring to pass.

The same thing is to be deduced from some words of Jesus a little later: 'And Jesus saith unto them, All ye shall be offended because of me this night:

for it is written, I will smite the shepherd, and the sheep shall be scattered' (Mk. 14:27). It is inevitable that the disciples will be 'offended'. There is a prophecy written concerning this and what is written in prophecy must be fulfilled.

The third example occurs when Jesus addresses those who had come to arrest him. 'I was daily with you in the temple teaching,' He said, 'and ye took me not: but the scriptures must be fulfilled' (Mk. 14:49). The arrest could take place and indeed must take place because certain scriptures were written about it. There is a necessity here. The scriptures *must* be fulfilled.

One could quote many instances of this kind. The citation of prophecy with respect to the passion is not peculiar to our Lord nor is it found only in the Gospels. It is found in all four Gospels and it is found also in the Acts and the Epistles. All the New Testament writers believed that the Old Testament was inspired of God, and that in its pages were many prophecies which found their fulfilment in the life and work of Jesus. Specifically they found many details of the passion prophesied. In the light of this fact what else could they conclude but that the death of their Lord took place fully in accordance with the will of their heavenly Father? The fulfilment of prophecy was clear evidence of the divine will. In other words the Father did not wait until the Son took action to save mankind. Before ever the Son appeared on earth the Father had decided to save men, and He inspired His servants the prophets to say so.

The same thing is implicit in the use of the word 'must' with respect to the sufferings of Jesus. Thus Matthew writes, 'From that time forth began Jesus to shew unto his disciples, how that he must go unto Jerusalem, and suffer many things. . .' (Mt. 16:21). The word 'must' carries with it an air of inevitability. There is a compelling divine necessity involved. It was not an accident that Jesus suffered. It was not simply that events being what they were, it turned out to be expedient that He should die for men. He *must* suffer. The necessity must be taken back to its origin in the will of God.

THE LOVE OF GOD

This is implicit also in the fact that God loves men. It is one of the basic Christian ideas about God that he is rightly called 'Father'. The very idea of a heavenly Father involves the thought of One who loves men and who is ready to provide for them. Whenever we say that God loves us, or whenever we refer to Him as our Father, or whenever we use any expression which implies His thought for us and His care for us, we are being reminded that the basic fact behind the whole Christian religion is that God loves us.

Now if God does love us it follows that the atonement proceeds from that love. It is impossible to reconcile the love of God with any view that God waits impassively while the Son brings about salvation. The fact that God loves us means that He takes the initiative in bringing about our salvation.

This is explicitly stated in a number of passages of Scripture. Probably the best known text in the whole of the Bible is John 3:16, 'For God so loved the world, that he gave his only begotten Son. . .' The point for us to notice is that this passage does not say that Jesus Christ showed His love for us in dying for us. It says that God, i.e. the Father, showed His love by giving His Son. And the same is the case elsewhere. 'God commendeth his own love toward us, in that, while we were yet sinners, Christ died for us' (Rom. 5:8, RV).

Now if we were not so used to it this would surely strike us as very surprising. If we tried to forget for one moment all that we have been told about the love of God and see Calvary as an isolated incident, it is very difficult indeed to associate it with divine love. On that cross hung a lowly carpenter from Nazareth. He had been betrayed by one of His close followers. He had been rejected by His own nation and handed over to the conquering Romans. He had been executed by the Romans, though the Governor quite evidently recognized His innocence. This was a travesty of justice if ever there was one. The whole shameful story is one of cowardice, self-interest, political expediency of the worst kind, and worse. Apart from the bearing of the Sufferer there is not one redeeming feature in the whole narrative.

Why should we think that the love of God is shown in such a miserable story? If we proceed along normal worldly lines of interpretation it is impossible to answer the question. Everything points to the sin of man. Nothing points to the love of God. Surely if God were loving He would intervene to save this Sufferer? If God were righteous and just would He not intervene to prevent this miscarriage of justice? But He does neither. He allows it to carry through to the bitter end.

Yet Christians have always maintained that the love of God *is* shown on the cross. Why? Surely the only possible answer is that God Himself is involved in what went on at Calvary. This is not something external to Him as though He were no more than a spectator. The reason why the love of God is shown in the cross is that there we see God Himself taking action for our sins. In the words of St. Paul, 'God was in Christ, reconciling the world unto himself' (II Cor. 5:19).

In the same passage, but a verse earlier, Paul puts a further emphasis on the work of God in Christ. He has been talking about the way in which the man who is 'in Christ' has become 'a new creation'. When any man puts his trust in Jesus Christ he becomes a different person. He finds a new power to overcome

51

evil and to walk in right ways. Sin is no longer the dominant factor in his life. Sin has been defeated. Having made his point that the old has disappeared and the new has come into being in such a man, Paul continues: 'From first to last this has been the work of God. He has reconciled us men to himself through Christ' (II Cor. 5:18, NEB).

It is important to be clear on this. Neither Paul nor any of the other New Testament writers speak of a salvation which takes place partly because man works it and partly because God works it. Salvation is the work of God alone. Throughout the New Testament the divine initiative receives strong stress. There is always the thought that God loves men, and that because he loves them He wills to save them. Salvation is a costly thing and it involves God sending His Son to the Cross. But He did this. He was determined to bring men salvation, and therefore He saw to it that all that was needed was done.

THE LOST SHEEP

The divine initiative is brought out powerfully in the trilogy of parables in Luke 15, the parable of the Lost Sheep, and the parable of the Lost Coin, and the parable of the Lost Son. In each of these the fact that salvation is all of God is brought out in one way or another.

For our present purpose the first of these three is perhaps particularly important. C. G. Montefiore has, in fact, gone on record as saying that this is the one thing in the teaching of Jesus to which he can find no parallel in the teaching of the rabbis.[1] It is true that among the rabbis one can find the virtues of repentance highly praised. At their best the rabbis give a moving picture of a God who is ready to receive the penitent sinner. Whenever a man truly turns from his sin and returns to God he can be sure of a welcome. But that is as far as the rabbis go.

In the parable of the Lost Sheep, however, Jesus goes further. He pictures for us a Father who does not simply wait until the lost decide to come back. Indeed part of the difficulty is that those who are thoroughly lost do not know how to get home. This parable teaches us that the Good Shepherd goes out looking for the sheep until he finds it and then he brings it home with him. The God of the New Testament is not a God who waits until men repent and then receives them back. He goes out actively to seek them and to bring them in. The divine initiative could scarcely be more strongly emphasized.

This is brought out also in the other two parables. In the parable of the Lost Coin the woman sweeps the house diligently until she finds the coin she had lost. The parable of the Lost Son does not perhaps, emphasize the divine initiative as strongly as the

[1] *The Synoptic Gospels* (London, 1927), vol. I, p. cxviii, vol. II, p. 520.

two preceding parables, but it does make it clear that salvation comes about because of what God does and not because of any merit in the saved. The prodigal son had no merit whatever. He had lost his all in the foreign country and when he came to his father he had no merit of any sort that he could claim. The parable is a powerful setting forth of the truth that men are saved on God's terms and not as the result of any merits or deservings of their own.

PREDESTINATION

The New Testament has a great deal besides this to say about the divine initiative, but we must pass over most of it. Let us, however, look for a moment at one more facet of it, namely predestination. This is not an aspect of New Testament teaching which commends itself to the modern world. We like to think that our wills are free, and that, for example, we decide for ourselves whether we will be saved or not. There is, of course, something in this. The New Testament never thinks of men as mere automata, pushed into compartments labelled 'saved' and 'lost' quite irrespective of their own desires in the matter. Salvation is not a mechanical process brought about without reference to the saved. Nevertheless to put the emphasis on the personal choice in the modern manner is quite unbiblical.

Throughout the New Testament it is insisted that man, left to himself, would much prefer to stay where he is in his sins. If he is to leave them it is necessary that he should be given strength to do so. Predestination means that God gives him that strength.

We might consider the words of Christ in which he says, 'No man can come to me, except the Father which hath sent me draw him' (Jn. 6:44). There cannot be the slightest doubt but that Jesus believed that some men had come to Him. These words indicate that they did not come because they themselves had chosen freely to do this. Basically they came because God gave them the strength to come, because God had 'drawn' them.

This thought is repeated many times in other parts of the New Testament. Thus Paul can say that the purpose of God is 'according to election. . . not of works' (Rom. 9:11). The doctrine of election is widespread in the New Testament and it signifies that God calls people to Himself. Every time we come up against this thought we are reminded of the priority of the divine. It is God, not man, who takes the initiative in this matter of salvation.

In the verse just quoted there is a reference to people being saved 'not of works'. It may be worth pointing out that this was a revolutionary discovery of the Christians. The first Christians were all Jews, but it was accepted in Judaism that salvation was of works. There might be some discussion as to precisely what works were required, but as to the fact that it

55

was works and not something else that brought man salvation there was no doubt.

It would not have been surprising if some of the less instructed Christians had carried on with this Jewish way of thought. In fact we read in Acts 15 of a serious discussion at high level with an assembly of apostles and presbyters to decide the matter, on whether Christians had to be circumcized and to agree to keep the whole law in the Jewish fashion. The assembly discussed the matter very thoroughly and came to the conclusion that the keeping of the Law is not required of Christians as the way of salvation. In other words the most solemn assembly of Christians recorded in the New Testament looked at the possibility of salvation by works and decided that this was not in accordance with Christian teaching. This means that salvation comes about in some other way, and in this context there cannot be any doubt as to what that other way is. It is the way of faith, which is the way of salvation through God's grace.

This in turn means that it is what God wills that is done. If men are saved not because of what they do, but because of what God does, then clearly the initiative is with Him. Thus whenever the New Testament tells us of God's free forgiveness, or of God's grace, or of men being saved by faith, or the like, there is always an emphasis on the priority of the divine grace.

From all this it seems very clear that throughout the New Testament there is a firm insistence on this truth that God saves men according to His own will. There is a divine initiative in this matter of salvation. The coming of Jesus Christ to die for men is not separate from the will of God but is an integral part of that divine will. In Gethsemane Jesus prayed, 'not my will, but thine, be done' (Lk. 22:42).

It is the consistent teaching of the New Testament that on Calvary God's will was done.

CHAPTER FIVE

CHRIST MEETS OUR NEED

BOOKS written on the atonement are legion. And there seem to be almost as many theories of the way in which the atonement 'works' as there are authors. It is an interesting fact that through the centuries the Church has agreed that the cross is at the very heart of the faith, but it has never come to an agreed conclusion as to how the cross saves men. Some Christians have thought of it as the means of God's winning a great victory. Some have seen in it a revelation of divine love. Some have regarded it as the payment of the debt that sinners owed. And we could go on. The theories are many, and the Church has never officially declared her mind on the matter.

One reason for all this is, I think, the complexity of the subject. Sin can be regarded from many aspects. It is at one and the same time a transgressing of God's law, a debt, an incurring of guilt, a coming under the power of some evil, and much more. Obviously anything that is able to deal effectively with all the aspects of all the sins of all men will itself be exceedingly complex. We must not expect it to be so simple that a child can understand it all. And when a thing is necessarily complex there is bound to be a certain amount of disagreement as to what it means essentially.

It seems to me that a recognition that the atonement is many-sided is a first essential if we are to make progess in the subject. A good deal of harm has been caused by well-meaning people who have had such a firm grasp of one aspect of the subject that they have proceeded to maintain that all else is immaterial. There is a well-known saying that 'Theories of the atonement are right in what they affirm and wrong in what they deny'. There is a certain amount of truth in this. It is not the whole truth. But it is certainly the case that quite often the positive contribution made by those who treat this subject is of value, while their denials of the force of other theories carry much less weight. This is not really surprising. Since the atonement is God's perfect provision for man's need it is necessarily many-sided. And since man's perception is at best partial each of us can perceive part of the truth only. Now the more clearly we perceive our one aspect of the truth the easier it is for us to be blind to other aspects. What we see is so right to us that we cannot but emphasize it. And when we do we are apt to miss what other people are seeing. From this it is but a step to denying that there is anything in their way of looking at it. We must always bear in mind that this subject is a large one, and that there are many ways of looking at it.

A REVELATION OF GOD'S LOVE

A view which goes back to Abelard (1079–1142), though it had to wait until quite recent times for its heyday, sees the essential thing about the atonement in the way it shows us the greatness of the love of God. The view, of course, did not originate with Abelard. It goes right back to the Bible, for we read, 'Herein is love, not that we loved God, but that he loved us, and sent his Son to be the propitiation for our sins' (I Jn. 4:10). What we owe to Abelard and the theologians who followed him is the development of this thought into a theory of the way the atonement works. According to this view there is no paying of a penalty or winning of a victory over the forces of evil (notice the denials!). The one thing that matters is that the cross shows us the love of God. We sinners look at the cross and are compelled to reflect that God really loves us very greatly. Christ endured such hostility from sinners, and that without murmur or complaint, without retaliation of any kind, that we can only marvel at the wonder of His love for us. Moved by this love we proceed to love God in return, and to loathe the sin which did such harm to the innocent Son of God. The effect of the cross accordingly is to be seen in the changed lives of those to whom it reveals the love of God.

The first thing to say about this theory is that it is true. Nothing shows us the love of God like the cross. We know the love of God in creation, and in the providence that watches over all men. But we do not know the depths of God's love until we see our Saviour laying down His life for men. 'Greater love hath no man than this, that a man lay down his life for his friends' (Jn. 15:13). The cross reveals God's love like nothing else does. And the cross inspires our devotion like nothing else does. It is impossible to contemplate Christ's death for us and remain unmoved. When we see that His death was not for any sins of His own (for He had none), but for ours, then we are grieved at that sin and we turn away from it. The cross is effective in inspiring us to right action.

We recognize this in our hymns. I suppose that the best known and best loved of all the hymns on the passion is 'When I survey the wondrous cross'. It is a hymn which speaks to the depths within us. We sing it with sincerity and complete conviction. But if you go through it carefully you will see that the only thing it tells us about the cross is that it has a profound effect on believers. The hymn is taken up exclusively with what we feel and do when we contemplate the cross.

The theory then is true. But it is also inadequate. For one thing it is not the death of Christ as such but His death for sin which shows us the love of God. The death by itself does not reveal anything. Someone has pointed out that if I am sitting quietly on the pier in the sunshine enjoying life and someone jumps into the water to prove his love for me and drowns I do not really see his point. Such a death is a revelation rather of folly than of love. If, however, I am caught in a raging torrent and someone at the risk of his life jumps in and pulls me out, then I can speak of a revelation of love. I was in danger. I have been saved at great risk. The greatness of the risk is the measure of the love.

Similarly if God loves us, if that love is such that He will surely forgive our sin and we are in no danger at all, then it is impossible to see how Christ's death shows His love. On this view the death of Jesus does nothing. It is not related to any reality. It is a piece of pageantry. The New Testament rather sees the love of God as shown in that He 'sent his Son to be the propitiation for our sins' (I Jn. 4:10). It is not the death, but the death for sin, the death which saves sinners from their sin, which shows us the love of God. We were in danger. We have been saved from our peril at great cost. That is what shows the love of God.

This theory really concentrates on man. It does not deal with the moral greatness of God, nor of His demands on man. It deals only with the effect on man of God's display of love. Man remains in the centre of the picture. But as James Denney points out, 'What pursues man in his sin and appeals to him is not love which is thinking of nothing but man, and is ready to ignore and to defy everything for his sake; it is a love which in Christ before everything does homage to that in God which sin has defied.'[1]

The truth is that this theory which concentrates on man fails to show us the love of God in its fulness, precisely because it does concentrate on man. It is only when we see that Christ in Denney's phrase is doing 'homage to that in God which sin has defied' that we really see God's love.

We welcome this theory then for what it has to tell us. We can never do without its emphasis on the divine love, nor its reminder that that love has effects in men's lives. But we cannot take it as the whole truth about the atonement, or even as the most significant truth about it. For that we must look elsewhere.

THE PERFECT EXAMPLE

The view that the effect of the cross is its effect on us is sometimes given precision in the suggestion that its primary function is to set us an example of patient suffering. Believers see in their Master's passion what real suffering means, and how men should endure it. They are therefore strengthened and encouraged to bear their own crosses through the world.

Evangelicals have always reacted against such views. They seem so inadequate in the light of the teaching of the New Testament as a whole that

[1] *The Christian Doctrine of Reconciliation*, London, 1918, p. 236.

those who claim to be scriptural in their understanding of doctrine often dismiss them out of hand. But this is too summary a proceeding. After all, the New Testament does speak of Christ as giving us an example in His death. Peter says explicitly, 'Christ also suffered for us, leaving us an example, that ye should follow his steps: who did no sin, neither was guile found in his mouth: who, when he was reviled, reviled not again; when he suffered, he threatened not; but committed himself to him that judgeth righteously . . .' (I Pet. 2:21 ff.).

There cannot be the slightest doubt that suffering is a part of life. We must suffer. But for Christians suffering has been transformed because of Christ's sufferings. They are the pattern for ours.[2] He was personally innocent and His death thus set the pattern for that suffering which is hardest of all to endure, suffering for something we have not done. Christ's example is of great force in such circumstances.

This must be insisted on, even though it also be insisted that Christians cannot follow Christ in the essential part of His sufferings. His death was vicarious. That is to say it was on behalf of others, and it

[2] Cf. A. M. Stibbs, 'He thus provided in principle a precedent and an *example* for His followers. Suffering is something in which all who would in this present world be associated with God's Christ, and be called "Christians", must expect to share. It is a prospect to be deliberately faced; and an experience to be regarded not with shame and resentment, but with joy and thanksgiving to God' (*Tyndale New Testament Commentaries*, *I Peter*, London, 1959, p. 117).

brings to others the blessing of forgiveness of sins. Our sufferings are not redemptive as were His. There are thus limits to the extent to which the view that Christ's sufferings were our example can be pressed. But within those limits the point is valid. He did show us how to suffer when we are unjustly accused. We must bear such suffering in the same spirit as He bore His.

CHRIST WON A VICTORY

One of the things the early Christian Fathers liked to do was to drive home the truth of the faith as they saw it by some vivid illustration. Sometimes they saw the atonement in ways which we can only regard as curious, but which obviously had a fascination for them.

They took sin seriously. They thought that because men have sinned they now rightly belong to Satan. When they leave this life they must go to hell. That is the due reward for their misdeeds. But God, the Fathers thought, made a bargain with Satan. God offered to let Satan have Jesus Christ, if he would release the souls of believers. Satan realized that this would represent a great gain to him, so he agreed eagerly. Calvary was the means whereby Christ was handed over. But then Satan found that he had overreached himself. He could get Christ down to hell when the Father handed Him over, but he could not keep Him there. On the first Easter Day Christ rose triumphant. He burst the bonds of hell and broke free. He returned to heaven whence He came and Satan was left lamenting. He had lost the souls he gave up in exchange for Christ, and he had lost Christ too.

It did not need a great deal of profound thought to see that God must have foreseen all this. His bargain with Satan looks to us suspiciously like a piece of deception and we think of it as unworthy. But this did not worry the Fathers at all. They saw in it proof of God's superior wisdom as well as His superior power. He could out-scheme Satan as well as defeat him in a test of strength.

One of the greatest of the early theologians, Gregory of Nyssa, likened the process of salvation to a fishing expedition. The deity of Christ was the fish-hook and His flesh the bait. Satan took the bait and was destroyed like any poor fish. And even Augustine of Hippo, surely one of the profoundest intellects of all time, improved on this only by substituting a mouse-trap for a fish-hook!

All this appears to us to be grotesque in the extreme. We find this talk of fish-hooks and mouse-traps repulsive, at any rate as a serious contribution to theology. We simply cannot think of God as acting in this way. It does not fit into our conception of a moral God, a God who loves justice and hates all iniquity. For this reason this aspect of the Fathers' thought was dismissed as unworthy of serious consideration until quite recently. But Gustav Aulen, a Swedish theologian, has in recent years pointed out that with all its naïvety and grotesqueness there was something valuable in this line of approach. The Fathers had at any rate a firm hold on the fact that in His death Christ won a resounding victory over all the forces of evil. On Calvary it appeared that wrong and wickedness had triumphed. But in fact that cross was the means whereby the greatest good was brought into the world. The defeat was illusory. The victory was real.

Aulen was able to go on and show that this note of victory has never ceased entirely in the Church. It survives most obviously in our Easter hymns. These are noteworthy for the triumphant tone which rings through them. And in theologians like Luther, Aulen found many passages which stress this aspect of the atonement.

More and more the truth of this is being recognized. There may be more to the atonement than this, but this is certainly part of it. Christ did appear to be beaten on Calvary. But in fact He won a tremendous victory. Not evil, but Christ is ultimately triumphant.

This is especially noteworthy in the early chapters of Acts. It is plain from these that the resurrection made a powerful appeal to the first Christians. They gloried in the fact that Christ had conquered death. And this thought is taken up elsewhere. Thus St.

Paul can exult: 'O death, where is thy sting? O grave, where is thy victory? The sting of death is sin; and the strength of sin is the law. But thanks be to God, which giveth us the victory through our Lord Jesus Christ' (I Cor. 15:55–57). The victory won by Christ and made actual in the experience of His followers is without a doubt one of the major thoughts of the New Testament.

Like the other views we have been considering, this one can be over-stressed. In the judgment of many, Aulen himself is guilty of this, for he seems to see the atonement as nothing more than a victory won by God. If this is all there is to it, then we come perilously close to asserting that in the last resort might is right. God on this view appears to be more concerned with getting His own way than with moral realities. This is untrue to the New Testament and untrue to Christian experience. The New Testament makes it clear that God has a concern for the moral law, and Christians know in their own experience that it is only when they have clear consciences that they can experience fellowship with God. To have defeated an enemy is not enough. God is not that kind of god.

There is also the point that as a final explanation of what the cross means this view lacks precision. How does a death on the cross followed by a resurrection involve the overthrow of evil? The answer is not obvious. Nor is it quite clear who or what 'the forces of evil' which Christ has overcome are. Some point out that if Aulen has in mind a personal devil, the evil one is astonishingly alive for a gentleman who has been slain. This is, of course, a difficulty on any theory, but it is an especial difficulty on a theory which puts all the stress on victory. And if it is not a personal devil that is in mind, but the evil dispositions within our hearts, then this view resolves itself into a variant of the first, that the effect of the atonement lies in its effects on the beholders. It energizes us to triumph over the evil within and the temptations without. In this case the theory has not only all the virtues but also all the defects of the view we considered at the start.

The theory then cannot be regarded as satisfactory if regarded as a complete explanation. But when it is seen as one aspect of the truth it has a permanent and a valuable place. Christ *did* win a victory, and those who are His know that victory in their own lives (Phil. 3:10). This is one of the precious things about the atonement. It is not simply a theoretical doctrine, but something which the believer proves true in his own experience day by day. Christ's victory gives us confidence as we live out our lives. We are confronted on every hand by forces of evil that are stronger than we are. But we do not despair. We know that Christ is stronger still. He defeated even death itself. And strong in His strength we can overcome the evil that confronts us.

From the time of the Reformation the legal aspects of the atonement have received special stress. It seemed to the Reformers crystal clear that sinners have put themselves in great danger because of their sin. 'The wages of sin is death' (Rom. 6:23), and the sinner can look forward to nothing else (and nothing less). God, the Reformers felt, is a moral God. He cannot trifle with His own holiness. He simply cannot regard the moral law as no more than a bye-law to be set aside if He wants to forgive. Moral considerations matter and God will not and cannot say otherwise.

But God is a God of love and it is His will to save men. Therefore He takes steps to save in a way that will uphold the moral law. Salvation involved the Son of God in coming to earth to live among men and then finally to die on the cross that death which is the wages of sin. In other words, Christ took our penalty upon Him and because He bore it we do not. In this way the just claims of the law are not overlooked, but at the same time men are not left to suffer the eternal consequences of their misdoings.

This is the teaching of one of the greatest New Testament passages on the cross, namely Romans 3:21–26. In this passage St. Paul speaks of 'the righteousness of God' as being manifested 'without the law'. The expression, 'the righteousness of God' appears to mean sometimes, 'the righteousness which God has', and sometimes, 'the righteousness which is from God', i.e. a righteousness which man has, but has only as a gift from God. This is certainly the meaning when the apostle refers to 'the righteousness of God which is by faith of Jesus Christ unto all and upon all them that believe' (v. 22). This is a righteousness which God bestows on believers, and 'righteousness' in this sense must mean 'standing as righteous', for righteousness as an ethical quality cannot be bestowed. By faith then men receive this 'right standing' in God's sight.

The apostle immediately goes on to indicate that there was need for this. 'All', he tells us, 'have sinned, and come short of the glory of God' (v. 23). This is the fact to which we drew attention in an earlier chapter. Men cannot secure 'right standing' in God's sight by their own efforts. They cannot live enough lives. They are doomed if they rely on their own efforts.

But they may be 'justified freely by his grace through the redemption that is in Christ Jesus' (v. 24). 'Justified' is a word which refers once again to 'right standing'. We can see this in the way we still use the term. If our conduct has been criticized and we set out to 'justify' ourselves, we do not set in motion a process of reforming our character or anything like that. We try rather to show that all along we have been in the right. As regards this accusation we set out to demonstrate our 'right standing'. We are not guilty. We are innocent.

And that is the way the term was used in the early centuries. Actually it was a legal term, and it belongs to the terminology of the law courts. It signified 'to acquit', 'to declare "Not guilty" '. There is not the slightest difficulty in showing that this use of the term was the regular one. It may be sufficient to quote a classical passage from the Old Testament, which deals with the action to be taken when there is a legal controversy. 'If there be a controversy between men, and they come unto judgment, that the judges may judge them; then they shall justify the righteous, and condemn the wicked' (Deut. 25:1). The duty of the judges is plain. They are to 'justify', i.e. to 'declare "Not guilty" ' the righteous and contrariwise to condemn the wicked. There can be no doubt as to the meaning of the term. And this passage is typical. The justification had its home in the law court. It was used quite widely outside legal matters, but it was the law court which gave it its significance (being like our term 'judge' in this)[3].

When St. Paul then speaks of being 'justified' he is referring to the way in which sinful men acquire their 'right standing' in the sight of God. This comes about 'freely', which means 'free of all charge', 'in the manner of a gift'. Men do not earn their 'right

[3] There is much more to be said about justification, and there are many disputes about both the significance of the term and the way it should be used in Christian theology. I have examined the subject more fully in my *The Apostolic Preaching of the Cross* (London, 1955), chapters VII, VIII.

standing' by their own efforts, such as leading a good
life. The apostle has just pointed out that all are
sinners, so that they cannot do this. If they are to be
justified before God it must be in some other way.
So he tells us that it is in the manner of a gift. Then
he puts the same thing in other words, 'by his
grace'.

The apostle proceeds to use other imagery. He says
that God set forth Christ 'to be a propitiation
through faith in his blood, to declare his righteousness for the remission of sins that are past ...
to declare, I say, at this time his righteousness:
that he might be just, and the justifier of him which
believeth in Jesus' (vv. 25 f.). 'Propitiation' refers
to the putting away of the wrath of God, that just
anger which is the divine reaction to sin. This was
done by the death of Jesus. Paul proceeds to the
point that it is the cross that shows God to be just,
and shows Him to be just in the very act whereby
He justifies the believer. The forgiveness of the
sinner is an act of mercy, but it is not in itself an act
of justice. Indeed some forms of forgiveness can be
terribly unjust. But God's concern for justice comes
out at the very same time as His concern to forgive
men. Paul is not saying, as some would have us believe, that God is shown to be a just God by the fact
that He saves men. The God who made men made
them so that it is possible for them to sin; and He
would not be just, so this reasoning runs, if He did

not also make provision for men to be saved when they did sin.

Whatever be the truth of this proposition, it is not what Paul is saying. He is saying that it is the *way* God saves men, not the *fact* that He saves them, that shows Him to be just. In other words salvation by the way of the cross shows God's concern for the moral law as well as His concern for men's salvation. He upholds the law at the same time as He saves sinners.

I do not see how it can be disputed that this is the teaching of the New Testament. The legal terminology of justification is quite frequent, and it is reinforced by sayings which use different imagery such as, 'Christ hath redeemed us from the curse of the law, being made a curse for us' (Gal. 3:13), or, 'he hath made him to be sin for us, who knew no sin; that we might be made the righteousness of God in him' (II Cor. 5:21). This imagery may not be congenial to many twentieth century men, but it made a strong appeal to the first Christians. They had no objection at all to saying that salvation has its legal aspect and that this aspect is important.

Sometimes in Protestant theology this aspect of the atonement has been overstressed. Some have spoken as though all that happened on Calvary was that our penalty was paid by Christ. This makes for a simple understanding of the atonement, and the uncomplicated always makes an appeal. But to take up this position is to overlook a great deal that the New Testament says. We have already noticed that the atonement may be seen as a revelation of God's love, as our example, and as a victory over evil, and there are other ways of seeing it that we have not touched on. When all this is taken into account it is clear that the atonement is not simply a paying of penalty. There is more to it than that.

There is also the fact to be considered that when all the emphasis is placed on the paying of penalty it is fatally easy to give the impression that God is concerned only with justice. He is not so much anxious to forgive the sinner as to see that the law is upheld. The Bible, of course, puts in the first place His great love and His deep concern to save.

But when full allowance has been made for the excesses of some, it still remains that the New Testament has a good deal to say about the legal aspect of the atonement. Granted, the atonement means more than the paying of penalty. But when we have said that, we have not somehow disposed of the passages which speak of justification. They still remain. And they bear their witness to the truth that one important way of looking at the cross is that which sees in it a bearing of our penalty. Our salvation is legally valid as well as powerfully efficacious. The fact that there are other significant aspects of the cross should not blind us to the importance of this one. If we are to retain our faith in a moral God and believe that morality is at the heart of the universe, we cannot hold that the just desert of sin was overlooked in the means whereby our salvation was brought about. It is the cross, seen as a process of justification, which safeguards this truth. In this universe debts are paid. The moral law is no mere chimera. Law as well as love is eternally significant.

CHRIST OUR SACRIFICE

In the familiar words of the consecration prayer in the Book of Common Prayer, on the cross Christ made '(by his one oblation of himself once offered) a full, perfect, and sufficient sacrifice, oblation, and satisfaction, for the sins of the whole world'. In the modern world we still use the language of sacrifice, but our understanding of it is different. We think rather of doing something at personal cost, for example when we speak of the sacrifices that poor parents must make to secure a good education for their children, or when we refer to the soldiers who die in the war as making the supreme sacrifice. This may be a legitimate way of using the term, but it does not give us the key to the New Testament use.

There we have rather the system of animal sacrifice in mind. Throughout the world of antiquity sacrifice was the almost universal religious rite. Among the Jews the procedure was as follows. A man would take along an animal to the altar, lay his hands on its head and then solemnly kill it. The priest would collect the blood, sprinkle some of it in a prescribed manner and pour the rest of it at the base of the altar. Then he would take certain prescribed parts of the animal (the whole of it in the case of the burnt sacrifice) and offer it to God in the flames of the altar. Finally the priest would dispose of the rest of the carcase according to the rules governing the particular sacrifice being offered. Sacrifice might express homage to God, or fellowship before God with other worshippers, or it might be concerned mainly with the expiation of sin.

When Christ is said to be a sacrifice for the sins of the whole world it is, of course, the sin offering that primarily is in mind. The way in which this worked is never recorded for us in the literature of antiquity and we are left to draw our inferences from what was done. As we have just seen, what was done was that the animal was brought to the altar, hands were laid on it (in New Testament times this appears to have been accompanied by the confession of the worshipper's sins), the animal was slain, its blood was sprinkled, and the carcase disposed of. Until recent times this has always seemed to scholars to indicate that the animal bore the sins of the worshipper and suffered in his stead. God was graciously pleased to accept the death of the animal in place of that of the sinner.

In recent times many scholars have been saying that sacrifice and death are not necessarily linked.

They point out that there are some grounds for thinking that the expression 'the blood' (often used in connection with the sacrifices) points to life rather than to death. They further contend that there were some sacrifices, such as the cereal offering, which were of material objects where death has no place.

Now it seems to me that a lot of loose thinking has gone into some of these modern theories. I have given all the biblical examples of the use of the term 'blood' a close scrutiny,[4] and this leaves me in no doubt but that the idea expressed by the term is that of a life yielded up in death, and not that of life. In any case I do not quite see what is meant when people say that the essence of sacrifice is the offering of life rather than death. That sacrifice for sin means the suffering of death as a penalty is intelligible. That it means the release of life is not. How does the release of life put away sin ? The answer is not obvious.

Nor am I very impressed with the putting forward of inanimate sacrifices like the cereal offering. Such sacrifices did indeed take place, but in every case they represent the destruction of the thing sacrificed as far as the worshipper is concerned. And in any case it must be borne in mind that such sacrifices were not commonly sacrifices for sin. As the writer to the Hebrews reminds us, 'almost all things are by the

[4] *The Apostolic Preaching of the Cross* (London, 1955), ch. III.

law purged with blood; and without shedding of blood is no remission' (Heb. 9:22). To put away sin it was enjoined that blood be shed, and the shedding of blood points to death.

The use of sacrifice then as a means of interpreting Christ's death signifies that Christ has borne our sins in His death. He is 'the Lamb of God, which taketh away the sin of the world' (Jn. 1:29); 'now once in the end of the world hath he appeared to put away sin by the sacrifice of himself' (Heb. 9:26); He 'offered one sacrifice for sins for ever' (Heb. 10:12). Such passages make it quite clear that in the judgment of the New Testament writers Jesus' death was the sacrifice which ended all sacrifices. Animal sacrifices in fact could not put away sins at all ('it is not possible that the blood of bulls and of goats should take away sins', Heb. 10:4). The most they could do was make 'a remembrance' of sins (Heb. 10:3). They indicated the way, but they could not take it. But what the animal sacrifices could not do Christ's sacrifice of Himself perfectly accomplished. His death really did put away sin.

We have not exhausted the subject. Many New Testament passages, for example, speak of redemption. This was a process whereby a price was paid and a person was set free either from slavery or from a death sentence. Or again, there are references to the 'new covenant' which Christ established with His blood. This brings to mind the occasion when Moses led the people in a covenant-making ceremony in which they solemnly undertook to discharge all the obligations involved in being the people of God (Ex.24). The prophets complained that the people did not keep the covenant and they looked forward to a time when God would make a new covenant, this time based on forgiveness of sins, and with the law of God not left as a series of external ordinances but as something written in the heart (Jer. 31:31 ff.). The men of the New Testament saw Jesus as bringing in this new covenant by the shedding of His blood. The cross was clearly right at the centre of Christianity for the early church, and the first preachers delighted to use a great variety of imagery as they tried to bring out the deep significance of it.

It is difficult, as we have said, for Christians to give a complete account of the atonement, and it is not really surprising that so many theories have been evolved. The reality is vast and deep and all our understandings of it are but partial. Harm is done when it is insisted—as it often has been in the past, and still is in some quarters in the present—that any one theory covers all the facts. The great fact on which the New Testament insists is that the atonement is many-sided and therefore completely adequate for every need. Do we appear as guilty sinners deserving death? Our death penalty has been borne. Are we enslaved to sin? The price has been paid and we are redeemed. Are we unable to realize the greatness of the love of God? The cross reveals it as nothing else can. Do we need an example to show us the way to go? Christ gives us that example in His death.

So we might go on. However we understand man's plight, the New Testament sees the cross as God's complete answer. Whatever needed to be done to put away our sin and to make us safe for all eternity He has done. The atoning work is satisfying and complete.

CHAPTER SIX

OUR RESPONSE

WE have been concerned to insist that in New Testament teaching the cross is at the very centre of
salvation. We all of us are sinners. Left to ourselves
none of us would ever attain salvation. But we are
not left to ourselves. The Son of God came to earth
and lived among men. Finally He died on Calvary's
cross, died that death which effectively puts away
the world's sins and opens up to men the gates of
everlasting life. But that does not mean, as some
optimistically assume, that salvation must necessarily
now come to all of us. It means that the way is open
wide, and that the invitation may be given, as it is
given in the concluding chapter of the Bible, 'who-
soever will, let him take the water of life freely'
(Rev. 22:17). But if the invitation is to be effective it
must be answered. A response is called for from those
for whom Christ died.

In different parts of the New Testament this response is expressed in various ways. But there seem
three things which are fairly constantly sought,
namely repentance, faith and godly living.

It is not without interest that the very first words

recorded in the preaching of our Lord, and of John the Baptist and of the apostles, are 'Repent: for the kingdom of heaven is at hand' (Mt. 4:17; 3:2; Mk. 6:12). Repentance is the fundamental demand. This is fairly obvious, for unless we forsake sin we have not begun to understand what Christianity is all about. Since Christ gave His life to save men from their sins, His followers cannot continue in their comfortable sins, going on their way untroubled. Rather they will heed the injunction of St. Paul, 'Let this mind be in you, which was also in Christ Jesus' (Phil. 2:5), and that with respect to sin as well as to other matters.

Repentance is not a meritorious work. We ought not to let a doctrine of salvation by works sneak in by the back door, by elevating repentance into a work which is pleasing in God's sight and which will accordingly be suitably rewarded. It is not meritorious in this sense at all. Rather it is the abandonment of any reliance on merit. It is the recognition that there is no merit or deserving in us, coupled with the resolve to forsake that which is evil.

This last point is important. Some people confuse repentance with remorse. The latter is a grieving over sin, and it may indeed be a most painful grieving. But it stops short at sorrow for the past. It does not include a determination to forsake the evil thing and as far as possible to overcome its effects. But this is characteristic of repentance. To be sorry that one has sinned is not enough. One must also be ready to turn from that sin and to walk in the ways of the Lord. Unless we have this attitude we have not begun to understand what salvation means.

It is further to be noted that repentance is an integral part of salvation by grace, though it is not nearly so necessary where men hold that salvation is by works. In the latter case it is held that what is essential is to see to it that one does more good than bad, to ensure that one's good deeds outweigh the bad, to keep one's account in credit in the heavenly ledger, as it were. When this is done there is no need to bother about some comparatively trivial offence. For that matter one can indulge from time to time in a fairly weighty sin, so long as the good deeds are there to outweigh it. I do not mean, of course, that anyone ever reasons it all out in this way. But the attitude is there. Where men believe that salvation stems from what they themselves do, they invariably hold that a few sins are neither here nor there. It may well be that that is the reason for some of the low standards today. There cannot be any doubt that most men in our communities today who believe in an after-life believe also that their own effort determines their destination. 'If you lead a good life you'll go to heaven when you die' sums up the popular view. And holding it they are not concerned about the trifle of evil which is all that they see in themselves. According to their own standards they are leading 'good' lives, and therefore they need not bother about a sin or two. Which inevitably leads sooner or later to a lowering of the standard to that which one can comfortably reach.

But the true Christian idea is quite different. For the Christian it is quite impossible to attain to heaven by one's own efforts. That comes about only through what Christ has done. And therefore the believer will turn away from *every* evil thing. It is not, for him, a question of balancing a certain amount of good against a corresponding amount of evil and then adding a bit of good to turn the scales. He sees that it was sin, his sin, that brought the sinless Son of God to the cross. His response is to turn away from every evil thing. He can never acquiesce in a situation when any remnant of evil remains. Wholehearted repentance is the necessary response when a man really begins to understand what Calvary is about.

FAITH

But it is not enough to forsake sin in repentance. The Christian is one who is characterized by his attitude to Christ. He lives his life by faith. As St. Paul puts it, 'the life which I now live in the flesh I live by the faith of the Son of God, who loved me, and gave himself for me' (Gal. 2:20). This makes faith not simply a comparatively unimportant part of the living out of the Christian Life. It places it right at the centre. To believe and to be a Christian are synonymous terms.

We must here guard against the same misconception as we saw in the case of repentance. Faith is not a good work. It is not that God saw that leading a good life is rather too hard a way for men to earn their salvation so provided that they should have the easier way of producing faith instead. There appear to be people who regard faith as meritorious, but this is not the view of the Bible. Faith there is the attitude which abandons trust in any human merit, not one which finds an acceptable substitute for the virtues which prove so elusive. Faith means casting oneself unreservedly on the grace of God. Faith means a realization that one has no merit in the sight of God, nothing at all to which to cling, save the very mercy of God Himself.

As old as the New Testament is another misconception about faith, namely that it may be set in opposition to good works, so that the believer need not bother how he lives. St. James complains of those who say that they have faith, but who have no good works to back up their faith. 'If a brother or sister be naked, and destitute of daily food, and one of you say unto them, Depart in peace, be ye warmed and filled; notwithstanding ye give them not those things which are needful to the body; what doth it profit? Even so faith, if it hath not works, is dead, being alone' (Jas. 2:15–17). This is not a denial of the critically important place of faith. James shows throughout his epistle that he values faith (Jas. 1:6, 2:1,5, 5:15), and in this very passage he can say, 'I will shew thee my faith by my works' (Jas. 2:18). He is not concerned for a Christianity without faith. Rather he sees faith as so important that he labours to destroy the spurious faith which some were evidently professing. He insists that a faith without works is a dead faith, but he does not say one word against a live faith. Rather, as we have seen, he advocates it.

And so it is throughout the New Testament. Everywhere the demand for faith is insistent. When Paul and Silas were imprisoned in Philippi and the earthquake came in the middle of the night, the jailor, having brought them out of the prison said, 'Sirs, what must I do to be saved?' And they said, 'Believe on the Lord Jesus Christ, and thou shalt be saved' (Acts. 16:30 f.). What is explicit here is implicit throughout the whole New Testament. The terminology may vary, but the basic attitude remains. The constant demand made on those who seek salvation is that they should believe.

For belief is a personal trust in a living Saviour. It means that Christ is seen as the only Saviour, as the only one who can deliver. Faith is a cry from the despair of realizing that there is no prop and stay to be found anywhere else. Faith is a cleaving to Christ with all one's heart. The New Testament knows no other door into salvation than the door that is opened by faith.

One of the interesting features of New Testament teaching on the way men live is that it insists with the greatest firmness on two almost opposite truths: that men are not saved by any good works whatever, and that the saved are men who are characterized by good works.

The first of these points we have tried to document in the earlier parts of this book. It is fundamental to the whole Christian understanding of the cross. Unless it is true there is no need for atonement. It is because men cannot save themselves by their good works that God sent His Son to be their Saviour.

But the second is also important. We ought not to think that the death of Christ is something which leaves those who believe untouched. On the contrary it affects them profoundly. The New Testament not only speaks of men as believing in Christ, but it also uses a number of other terms to designate the process whereby they become Christian. Sometimes this is seen as conversion, or again as a being born again, or as being made partakers of the divine nature. The New Testament writers may speak of the change as so radical that they refer to a death to the old way and a rising to a new. They speak of being buried with Christ and of being raised with Him. They refer to putting off the old man and putting on the new. They can say that if a man is in Christ there is a new creation.

All this must be taken with the utmost seriousness. For the first Christians the atonement is not seen as a way of excusing men from the tremendous moral demands that God makes on them. Rather it is only in the light of the atonement that those moral demands can be seen in all their fulness and met even approximately. Only as we appreciate that Christ had to die to put away our sin can we see sin for the enormity it is. Only then can we understand that certain things *are* sins, and therefore only then can we really grasp the magnitude of the moral demands that God makes on us.

But when we have seen these moral demands, when we have seen that we cannot meet them and that Christ has made the provision for our salvation, we have not thereby got rid of them. They are still there. But now we see that we are to face them, not as those who try laboriously to achieve salvation for themselves by their strenuous efforts, but rather as those who respond joyfully to what Christ has done. The Christian delights to live his life with a single eye to the glory of God, not because he hopes to deserve salvation thereby but because he knows he cannot. He lives now as one who has been redeemed by the Lord. He lives to do the service of his Saviour. Good works are the response to the salvation he has received, not a means of bringing it about. They are the fruit of his salvation, not its root. They are its inevitable consequence, not its cause.

These good works that the Christian does, he does not do in his own strength. It is fundamental to the Christian approach to life that those who have been saved by Christ have access to the infinite resources of God Himself as they seek to live out the implications of their faith. God sets His Spirit within them, so that it can be said, 'as many as are led by the Spirit of God, they are the sons of God' (Rom. 8:14; cf. also v. 9, 'if any man have not the Spirit of Christ, he is none of his'). The other religions of antiquity were familiar with the thought that a divine spirit might come and dwell in men, but they always restricted this to a select group of specially favoured men. It was a revolutionary idea of the Christians that God gives His Spirit to all believers. It was a further revolutionary idea that the presence of the Spirit is not to be discerned in curious behaviour of the 'whirling dervish' type, but in ethical conduct: 'the fruit of the Spirit is love, joy, peace, longsuffering, gentleness, goodness, faith, meekness, temperance' (Gal. 5:22 f.).

This ought not to be thought of as something separate from the atonement. It is separable for purposes of discussion. But the man whose sins are forgiven by Christ is also the man in whom God has set His Spirit, the man of whom God asks that he live an upright life. To put the same thing in another way, Christians are saved to serve. Service is not a curious consequence that happens in the case of a few odd souls, but the normal thing for every believer. Redemption means not simply that we are delivered from the unpleasant consequences of sin. It means that we are freed from sin's dominion and that we now must live as those who are free. 'Ye are bought with a price', writes Paul, 'therefore glorify God' (I Cor. 6:20).

THE CROSS IS CENTRAL

From all this it is clear that in the New Testament view the cross is absolutely central. It is the means of bringing us salvation and it is the basis of our living the saved life. It is, or should be the burden of all our preaching. A Christianity which is not cross-centred is not Christianity at all.

This is of the utmost importance both for our understanding of the faith and for our proclamation of it. It is a weakness of much modern preaching that the cross is scarcely mentioned. But in the history of the Christian Church it is when the cross has been preached boldly and clearly that preaching has had power. The great preachers, like the great theologians, have gloried in the cross, and they have set it forth as God's answer to men's need. And when they have done so the power of the cross to save has always been vindicated.

It is true some have preached the cross in such a way as to give offence and repel men. But some preachers can give offence whatever they preach. The man, not the message, is at fault. Such men can so preach the cross as to make God appear a narrow tyrant. They offer such a repellent view of the atonement that only those who are prepared to sacrifice their intellect can be saved. But this is not preaching the cross. It is preaching a private interpretation without biblical foundation. For it is also possible to preach the cross in such a manner that men are attracted. Men are still saved today by the authentic message of the cross.

Nevertheless it must be borne in mind that there is such a thing as 'the offence of the cross' (Gal. 5:11). The cross is not a message of human origin. Men did not think it up for themselves. Indeed, in their 'wisdom' men may well think that the message of the cross is foolishness (I Cor. 2). In this sense there is an offence about the cross which cannot be avoided. But in the last resort Christians must bear in mind that the message they are to proclaim is God-given. It is not for them to alter it, whether they are pleased with it or not. The fact that many in our day dislike the message of Christ crucified does not mean that it is out of date and must be abandoned. It means that the unspiritual are running true to form. In every age they have rejected the cross and we have no reason for thinking that it will be otherwise in our own day.

We cannot take these rejecters of the gospel as our standard and tailor our message until it becomes acceptable to them. We must preach Christ crucified, for that is the central content of the gospel. Whether they accept it or whether they reject it we must preach the cross. But in fact, when this is done, men still respond. Men's need in the latter part of the twentieth century is the same as ever it was, and the message of the cross meets that need as fully now as ever it did.

It is worth reflecting that Paul had to face the problem of the essential content of his message. He was confronted by some who demanded that Christians should be circumcized and taught to keep the entire law of Moses in true Jewish style. This challenged him. What was he doing as he preached Christ? Was Christianity no more than a revised and up-to-date Judaism? Did it call for men to submit to ordinances like circumcision? And to seek merit in the keeping of God's commandments? His answer, which is developed in the Epistle to the Galatians, was that such a course would be no more than a glorying in the flesh. He could say, 'But God forbid that I should glory, save in the cross of our Lord Jesus Christ, by whom the world is crucified unto me, and I unto the world. For in Christ Jesus neither circumcision availeth anything, nor un-circumcision, but a new creature' (Gal. 6:14 f.).

The position remains the same to this day. Neither submission to circumcision (or for that matter to any other rite, sacramental or otherwise) nor the refusal to submit will help us when we stand before God. What will matter then is what Paul calls 'a new creature', that new creative work that is accomplished in the redeemed through the activity of the crucified Lord. Since this is a creative work done by Him man can take no credit for it. Man is left with nothing to glory in save the cross.

The cross then is not something to be apologized for, but something to glory in and blazon abroad. As we preach it we may know that we are holding out to men the salvation that God sent His Son to win. The preacher of any other message may well hesitate and tremble. He is offering the wisdom of men and it may not prove adequate. But he who preaches 'Christ, and him crucified' can do so with complete assurance. The cross has been the means of bringing men salvation through the centuries and it is still doing so. It is still God's answer to that most intract-able of human problems, the problem of sin. Preaching that exalts Christ crucified can still be dynamic, the very power of God unto salvation for every one who believes.

There is glory in the cross.